SYLLABUS STANDARD 8

YEARLY PLANNER FOR ACADEMIC YEAR 2022-23

AASHISH

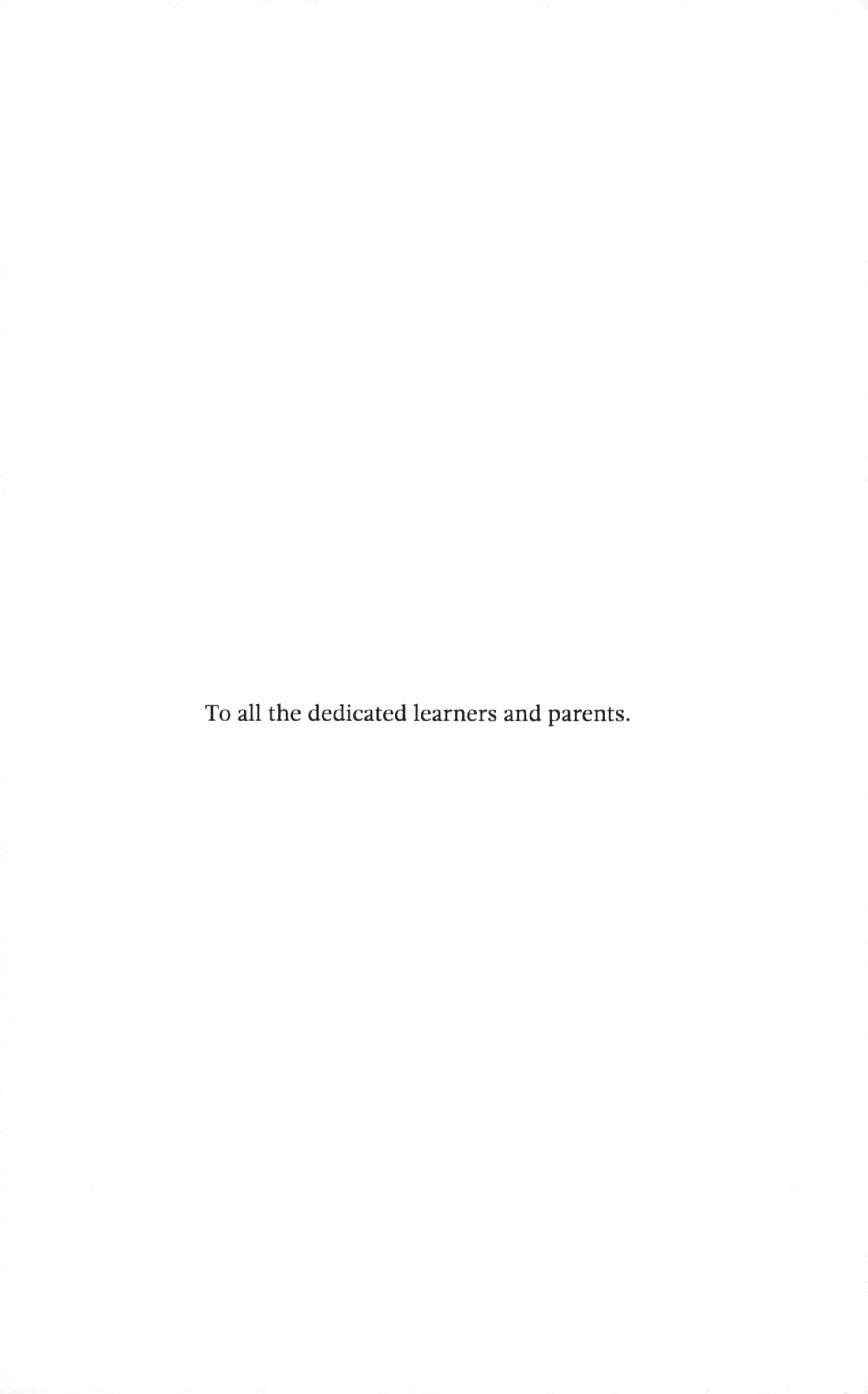

To all the dedicated learners and parents.

Contents

Foreword

I believe that education shapes the character, calibre and prospect of an individual. Education has no perimeter to restrict. Intensive and critical thinking, sharpening intelligence, refining character – all are a part of dignified education. Students of Heavenly Blessings Academy are benefitted by such type of education.

Preface

This book contains complete syllabus for Class 8 CBSE for the subjects of English, Mathematics, Science and Social Science. It also contains paper patterns and Marks wise weightage for every lesson of all the subjects.

Yearly planner is also mentioned at last.

Few additional activities that will be conducted this year:

HBPL Season 3: Box Cricket Tournament.

Movie Time.

Trek Trip: If things go well with permissions.

Academic Competitions: Elocution, Debate, etc.

Book Writing Activity.

This year we would also provide extra books 'HB Spotlight' that will contain summarised lessons in lucid language, solutions to NCERT Textual Questions, Extra Important Mark wise Questions, Important MCQ and lots more.

Why to select us?

Because all the costs are included in the fees and no extra cost will be incurred! Neither for the Andriod Application or for the Extra Books, Activities, Tests, Trips, Practicals, ID cards, etc. etc. etc.

Acknowledgements

Special Thanks to my team of learners, motivators, friends, parents and Team Heavenly Blessings.

Prologue

My Goals This Year:

I will help to create a shared vision for students, staff and community members. I will take the time to gather input and knowledge from as many stakeholders as possible.

I will utilize my supervisory time to build and establish relationships with students and staff. I will talk with students and staff and ask them about their lives in a sincere and caring manner. I will take an active interest in learning as much as I can about them.

I will have high expectations for students, staff and myself. I will help to empower others to take control of their own learning and development by establishing an environment built on accountability and responsibility.

I will support and encourage those with whom I work. I will work to embrace a sharing and collaborative school culture that takes risks in an effort to do great things.

I will listen more than I talk. I will use my two ears more than I use my one mouth, and I will try to learn as much as I can from others. I will make it a priority to get into classrooms to observe on a daily basis, and I will learn by listening and observing.

I will communicate with and involve parents and community stakeholders as often as possible. I will work with teachers and staff to keep parents informed and up-to-date with what is going on in our school through the use of weekly newsletters, our school website and social media outlets.

I will share the power of my PLN with my colleagues. I will take the time to meet with anyone interested in learning more about using social media as a means toward professional growth. I will model being a lifelong learner for both students and staff.

I will have a healthy balance between my professional and personal life. Though I anticipate the high level of time commitment required for this job, I do not want my job to consume my entire life. My family, friends and colleagues will all benefit from this healthy balance.

I will base every decision I make on what is best for students. It is difficult to not get caught up in everything that is going on, but I will make every effort to put students and their needs first.

CHAPTER I

English Syllabus

CBSE Syllabus for Class 8 English (Honeydew – Textbook in English for Class VIII)

Chapter 1: The Best Christmas Present in the World
Poem: The Ant and the Cricket
Chapter 2: The Tsunami
Poem: Geography Lesson
Chapter 3: Glimpses of the Past
Poem: Macavity -The Mystery Cat
Chapter 4: Bepin Choudhury's Lapse of Memory
Poem: The Last Bargain
Chapter 5: The Summit Within
Poem: The School Boy
Chapter 6: This is Jody's Fawn
Poem: The Duck and the Kangaroo
Chapter 7: A Visit to Cambridge
Poem: When I set out for Lyonnesse
Chapter 8: A Short Monsoon Diary
Poem: On the Grasshopper and Cricket
Chapter 9: The Great Stone Face- I
Chapter 10: The Great Stone Face- II
CBSE Syllabus for Class 8 English (It So Happened – Supplementary Reader in English for Class VIII)

Chapter 1: How the Camel got his Hump
Chapter 2: Children at work
Chapter 3: The Selfish Giant
Chapter 4: The Treasure within
Chapter 5: Princess September
Chapter 6: The Fight
Chapter 7: The Open Window
Chapter 8: Jalebis

Chapter 9: The Comet- I

Chapter 10: The Comet- II

Chapter 11: Ancient Education System of India

Students can also access the syllabus for others subjects by visiting CBSE Class 8 Syllabus page.

CBSE Syllabus for Class 8 English Grammar

The English Grammar syllabus for CBSE Class 8 has the following topics:

a. Order of Words and Clauses

b. Direct and Indirect Speech

c. Active and Passive Voice

d. Tenses

e. Noun

f. Pronoun

g. Verb

h. Adverb

i. Prepositions

j. Conjunction

k. Phrases and Idioms

l. Vocabulary

m. Comprehension Reading

CBSE Syllabus for Class 8 English Composition (Writing)

This section tests your writing skills in English. The English Composition syllabus for CBSE Class 8 has the following topics:

a. Notice

b. Story

c. Formal and Informal Letters

d. Diary Entry

e. Essay

Overall this subject contains 10 lessons and 8 poems in Honey Dew and 11 Lessons in It So Happened.

English Paper Pattern

The CBSE Class 8 English question paper consists of 80 marks and is divided into three parts:

Section A: Reading	Consists of unseen comprehension passages under which are a reference to context questions for 1 mark each.
Section B: Writing and Grammar	This section consists of writing notices, letters and essays, and the grammar part has several fill in the blanks questions.
Section C: Literature	There are two kinds of questions in the literature section: • An excerpt of a poem or prose will be given along with several references to context questions. • 2 mark questions for about a paragraph each about the lessons from the literature textbook.

Marks Destribution

CHAPTER II

Mathematics Syllabus

The chapter in the NCERT Maths textbook are as per the syllabus. Students of CBSE Class 8 must cover the CBSE Syllabus for Class 8 by studying these chapters from the prescribed NCERT book.

Chapter 1: Rational Numbers

1.1 Introduction

1.2 Properties of Rational Numbers

1.3 Representation of Rational Numbers on the Number Line

1.4 Rational Number between Two Rational Numbers

Chapter 2: Linear Equations in One Variable

2.1 Introduction

2.2 Solving Equations which have Linear Expressions on one Side and Numbers on the other Side

2.3 Some Applications

2.4 Solving Equations having the Variable on both sides

2.5 Some More Applications

2.6 Reducing Equations to Simpler Form

2.7 Equations Reducible to the Linear Form

Chapter 3: Understanding Quadrilaterals

3.1 Introduction

3.2 Polygons

3.3 Some of the Measures of the Exterior Angles of a Polygon

3.4 Kinds of Quadrilaterals

3.5 Some Special Parallelograms

Chapter 4: Practical Geometry

4.1 Introduction

4.2 Constructing a Quadrilateral

4.3 Some Special Cases

Chapter 5: Data Handling

5.1 Looking for Information

5.2 Organising Data

15.1 Introduction

15.2 Linear Graphs

15.3 Some Applications

Chapter 16: Playing with Numbers

16.1 Introduction

16.2 Numbers in General Form

16.3 Game with Numbers

16.4 Letters for Digits

16.5 Test of Divisibility

Overall this subject contains 16 lessons.

For Mathematics, students will also be provided with NCERT Exemplar for prescribed extra questions practices.

Mathematics Paper Pattern

Lessonwise Weightage:

SR NO	NAME OF CHAPTERS	Term	1MARK	2MARKS	3MARKS	4MARKS	TOTAL
1	RATIONAL NUMBERS	I	-	2(1)	3(1)	-	**5(2)**
2	LINEAR EQUATION INONE VARIABLE		-	2(1)	-	4(1)	**6(2)**
3	UNDERSTANDING QUADRILATERALS		1(1)	2(1)	-	-	**3(2)**
4	PRACTICAL GEOMETRY		-	-	3(1)	-	**3(1)**
5	DATA HANDLING		-	-	3(1)	4(1)	**7(2)**
6	ALGEBRAIC EXPRESSIONS AND IDENTITIES	II	1(1)	2(1)	3(1)	4(1)	**10(4)**
7	VISUALISING SOLID SHAPES		1(1)	-	3(1)	-	**4(2)**
8	MENSURATION		1(1)	-	3(1)	4(1)	**8(3)**
9	EXPONENTS AND POWERS		1(1)	-	3(1)	4(1)	**8(3)**
10	DIRECT AND INDIRECT VARIATION		-	-	3(1)	4(1)	**7(2)**
11	FACTORISATION		1(1)	2(1)	-	4(1)	**7(3)**
12	INTRODUCTION TO GRAPHS		-	-	3(1)	4(1)	**7(2)**
13	PLAYING WITH NUMBERS		-	2(1)	3(1)	-	**5(2)**
	TOTAL		**6(6)**	**12(6)**	**30(10)**	**32(8)**	**80 (30)**

Mathematics Blueprint

CHAPTER III

Science Syllabus

Detailed NCERT Syllabus for Class 8 Science

The different topics included in each chapter are as under:

Chapter 1: Crop Production and Management

1.1: Agricultural Practices

1.2: Basic Practices of Crop Production

1.3: Preparation of Soil

1.4: Sowing

1.5 Adding Manure and Fertilizers

1.6: Irrigation

1.7: Protection from Weeds

1.8: Harvesting

1.9: Storage

1.10: Food from Animals

Chapter 2: Microorganisms: Friend and Foe

2.1: Microorganisms

2.2: Where do Microorganisms Live?

2.3: Microorganisms and Us

2.4: Harmful Microorganisms

2.5: Food Preservation

2.6: Nitrogen Fixation

2.7: Nitrogen cycle

Chapter 3: Synthetic Fibres and Plastics

3.1: What are Synthetic Fibres?

3.2: Types of Synthetic Fibres

3.3: Characteristics of Synthetic Fibres

3.4: Plastics

3.5: Plastics as Materials of Choice

3.6: Plastics and the Environment

Chapter 4: Materials: Metals and Non-Metals

4.1: Physical Properties of Metals and Non-metals

Chapter 9: Reproduction in Animals

9.1: Modes of Reproduction

9.2: Sexual Reproduction

9.3: Asexual Reproduction

Chapter 10: Reaching The Age of Adolescence

10.1: Adolescence and Puberty

10.2: Changes at Puberty

10.3: Secondary Sexual Characters

10.4: Role of Hormones in Initiating Reproductive Function

10.5: Reproductive Phase of Life in Humans

10.6: How is the Sex of the Baby Determined?

10.7: Hormones other than Sex Hormones

10.8: Role of Hormones in Completing the Life History of Insects and Frogs

10.9: Reproductive Health

Chapter 11: Force And Pressure

11.1: Force: A push or a Pull

11.2: Forces are due to an Interaction

11.3: Exploring Forces

11.4: A Force can Change the State of Motion

11.5: Force can Change the Shape of an object

11.6: Contact Forces

11.7: Non-contact Forces

11.8: Pressure

11.9: Pressure Exerted by Liquids and Gases

11.10: Atmospheric Pressure

Chapter 12: Friction

12.1: Force of Friction

12.2: Factors affecting Friction

12.3: Friction: A Necessary Evil

12.4: Increasing and Reducing Friction

12.5: Wheels Reduce Friction

12.6: Fluid Friction

Chapter 13: Sound

13.1: Sound is Produced by Vibrating Bodies

17.5: Some Other Members of the Solar System

Chapter 18: Pollution of Air and Water

18.1: Air Pollution

18.2: How does Air Get Polluted?

18.3: Case Study- The Taj Mahal

18.4: Greenhouse Effect

18.5: What can be done?

18.6: Water Pollution

18.7: How does Water Get Polluted?

18.8: What is Potable Water and How is Water Purified?

18.9: What Can be Done?

Overall this subject contains 18 lessons.

For Science, students will also be provided with NCERT Exemplar for prescribed extra questions practices.

Science Paper Pattern

Lessonwise Weightage:

S.NO.	CHAPTER	VSA (1mark)	SA-I (2marks)	SA-II (3marks)	LA (5marks)	Activity based (2marks)	TOTAL
1	CROP PRODUCTION AND MANAGEMENT		1 (2)				1(2)
2	MICRO ORGANISMS:FRIENDS AND FOE		1 (2)				1(2)
3	SYNTHETIC FIBRES AND PLASTICS		1 (2)				1(2)
4	MATERIALS: METALS AND NON-METALS		1 (2)				1(2)
5	COAL AND PETROLEUM		1 (2)				1(2)
6	COMBUSTION AND FLAME		1 (2)				1(2)
7	CONSERVATION OF PLANTS AND ANIMALS			1 (3)			1(3)
8	CELL:STRUCTURE AND FUNCTIONS			1 (3)			1(3)
9	REPRODUCTION IN ANIMALS			1 (3)			1(3)
10	REACHING THE AGE OF ADOLESCENCE			1 (3)			1(3)
11	FORCE AND PRESSURE	1 (1)		1 (3)		1 (2)	3 (6)
12	FRICTION	1 (1)		1 (3)		1 (2)	3 (6)
13	SOUND				1 (5)	1 (2)	2 (7)
14	CHEMICAL EFFECTS OF ELECTRIC CURRENT				1 (5)	1 (2)	2 (7)
15	SOME NATURAL PHENOMENA				1 (5)	1 (2)	2 (7)
16	LIGHT				1 (5)	1 (2)	2 (7)
17	STARS AND THE SOLAR SYSTEM			1 (3)	1 (5)		2 (8)
18	POLLUTION OF AIR AND WATER			1 (3)	1 (5)		2 (8)
	TOTAL	2 (2)	6 (12)	8 (24)	6 (30)	6 (12)	80

Science Blueprint

CHAPTER IV

Social Science Syllabus

The names of the chapters are listed here.

The CBSE Syllabus for Class 8 History is as under.

Chapter 1: How, When and Where

Chapter 2: From Trade to Territory: The Company Establishes Power

Chapter 3: Ruling the Countryside

Chapter 4: Tribals, Dikus and the Vision of a Golden Age

Chapter 5: When People Rebel

Chapter 6: Colonialism and the City

Chapter 7: Weavers, Iron Smelters and Factory Owners

Chapter 8: Civilising the "Native", Educating the Nation

Chapter 9: Women, Caste and Reform

Chapter 10: The Changing World of Visual Arts

Chapter 11: The Making of the National Movement: 1870s – 1947

Chapter 12: India after Independence

The CBSE Syllabus for Class 8 Geography is as under:

Chapter 1: Resources

Chapter 2: Land, Soil, Water, Natural Vegetation and Wildlife Resources

Chapter 3: Mineral and Power Resources

Chapter 4: Agriculture

Chapter 5: Industries

Chapter 6: Human Resources

The CBSE Syllabus for Class 8 Civics is as under:

Unit One: The Indian Constitution and Secularism

Chapter 1: The Indian Constitution

Chapter 2: Understanding Secularism

Unit Two: Parliament and the Making of Laws

Chapter 3: Why do we need a Parliament?

Social Studies Paper Pattern

Sr No	Name of Chapter	VSA=1 (Very Short Answers)	SA=3 (Short Answers)	LA=5 (Long Answers)	Map	Total
1	How, When and Where	---	---	---	---	---
2	From Trade to Territory	1(1)	---	---	---	1
3	Ruling the Countryside	---	---	1(5)or1(5)	---	5
4	Tribal, Dikus…	---	---		---	
5	When People Rebel	---	---	---	1(2)	2
6	Colonialism and the	---	---	---	---	---
5	Weavers ,Iron Smelters	---	1(3)	---	---	3
6	Civilising the Native…	1(1)	---	---	---	1
7	Women, Caste	---	1(3)	---	---	3
8	The Changing World of	2(1)	---	---	---	2
9	The Making of the National Movement	---	---	1(5)	---	5
10	India After Independence	---	---	1(5)	---	5
1	The Indian Constitution	---	---	1(5)	---	5
2	Understanding Secularism	---	---	---	---	---
3	Why do we need a Parliament	---	1(3)	---	---	3
4	Understanding Laws	---	---	---	---	---
5	Judiciary	---	---	---	---	---
6	Understanding Our Criminal Justice System	---	1(3)	---	---	3
7	Understanding Marginalisation	1(1)	1(3)	---	---	4
8	Confronting Marginalisation	---	1(3)	---	---	3
9	Public Facilities	---	1(3)	---	---	3
10	Law and social justice	---	---	1(5)	---	5
1	Resources or Agricultural	---	1(3) or 1(3)	---	---	3
2	Land, Soil, Water, Natural Vegetation and Wild Life Recourses	---	---	1(5)	---	5
3	Minerals and Power Resources	---	---	---	---	---
4	Industries	2(1)	1(3)	---	1(3)	8
5	Human Resources	---	2(3)	1(5)	---	11
		7(1)	11(3)	7(5)	1(5)	80

Social Science Blue Print

CHAPTER V

Overall View

Total Number of Lessons to be studied in the Academic Year 2022-23

Subject	Total Lessons
English	21
Mathematics	16
Science	18
Social Science	26
Total Lessons	**81**
Excluding Grammar and Writing Skills for English. They will be taught but is not included in this count.	

Total Number of Month wise Working Days

Month	Working Days	Total Weekend Test
April	26	4
May	**Complete Off**	
June	26	4
July	26	5
August	26	4
September	26	4
October	22	4
November	26	4
December	25	4
January	25	5
February	24	4
March	**Final Examination Revision**	
Total	254	42

Year Planner 2022-23

List of Holidays:

15th August: Independence Day

22nd October to 26th October: Diwali Vacations

26th January: Republic Day

Class Duration: 2 Hours Per Day

Timings will be decided with your consent.

Note that there are many tests planned based on JEE | NEET Pattern as well. All Month End Tests will follow JEE | NEET | MH-

CET Test Patterns.

First Weekend MCQ Tests will be conducted online on Heavenly Blessings Mobile Application to provide the practise of CPT pattern.

Second Weekend MCQ Test will be conducted offline.

Third Weekend MCQ Test will be conducted online on Heavenly Blessings Mobile Application based on JEE | NEET | MH-CET Pattern.

Fourth Weekend Test will be a subjective test. Subject will be informed timely.